APHRODITE
Goddess of Love and Beauty

Written by Teri Temple
and Maria Koran
Illustrated by Robert Squier

MEDIA ENHANCED BOOKS
AV²
BY WEIGL™
ADDED VALUE • AUDIO VISUAL

www.av2books.com

AV² provides enriched content that supplements and complements this book. Weigl's AV² books strive to create inspired learning and engage young minds in a total learning experience.

Your AV² Media Enhanced books come alive with...

Audio
Listen to sections of the book read aloud.

Key Words
Study vocabulary, and complete a matching word activity.

Video
Watch informative video clips.

Quizzes
Test your knowledge.

Embedded Weblinks
Gain additional information for research.

Slide Show
View images and captions, and prepare a presentation.

Try This!
Complete activities and hands-on experiments.

... and much, much more!

Go to www.av2books.com, and enter this book's unique code.

BOOK CODE

V442989

AV² by Weigl brings you media enhanced books that support active learning.

Published by AV² by Weigl
350 5th Avenue, 59th Floor
New York, NY 10118
Website: www.av2books.com

Printed in Brainerd, Minnesota, United States
1 2 3 4 5 6 7 8 9 0 20 19 18 17 16

072016
070416

Project Coordinator: Warren Rylands
Art Director: Terry Paulhus

Every reasonable effort has been made to trace ownership and to obtain permission to reprint copyright material. The publishers would be pleased to have any errors or omissions brought to their attention so that they may be corrected in subsequent printings.

Weigl acknowledges Getty Images and iStock as its primary image suppliers for this title.

Library of Congress Cataloging-in-Publication Data

Names: Temple, Teri, author.
Title: Aphrodite / Teri Temple.
Description: New York : AV² by Weigl, 2016. | Series: Gods and goddesses of ancient Greece | Includes index.
Identifiers: LCCN 2016003570 (print) | LCCN 2016004602 (ebook) | ISBN 9781489646316 (hard cover : alk. paper) | ISBN 9781489650368 (soft cover : alk. paper) | ISBN 9781489646323 (Multi-User eBook)
Subjects: LCSH: Aphrodite (Greek deity)--Juvenile literature. | Mythology, Greek--Juvenile literature. | Goddesses, Greek--Juvenile literature.
Classification: LCC BL820.V5 T46 2016 (print) | LCC BL820.V5 (ebook) | DDC 292.2/114--dc23
LC record available at http://lccn.loc.gov/2016003570

GODS AND GODDESSES OF ANCIENT GREECE

CONTENTS

INTRODUCTION

Long ago in **ancient Greece** and Rome, most people believed that gods and goddesses ruled their world. Storytellers shared the adventures of these gods to help explain all the mysteries in life. The gods were immortal, meaning they lived forever. Their stories were full of love and tragedy, fearsome monsters, brave heroes, and struggles for power. The storytellers wove aspects of Greek customs and beliefs into the tales. Some stories told of the creation of the world and the origins of the gods. Others helped explain natural events such as earthquakes and storms. People believed the tales, which over time became myths.

The ancient Greeks and Romans **worshiped** the gods by building temples and statues in their honor. They felt the gods would protect and guide them. People passed down the myths through the generations by word of mouth. Later, famous poets such as and Hesiod wrote them down. Today, these myths give us a unique look at what life was like in ancient Greece more than 2,000 years ago.

ANCIENT GREEK SOCIETIES

In ancient Greece, cities, towns, and their surrounding farmlands were called city-states. These city-states each had their own governments. They made their own laws. The individual city-states were very independent. They never joined to become one whole nation. They did, however, share a common language, religion, and culture.

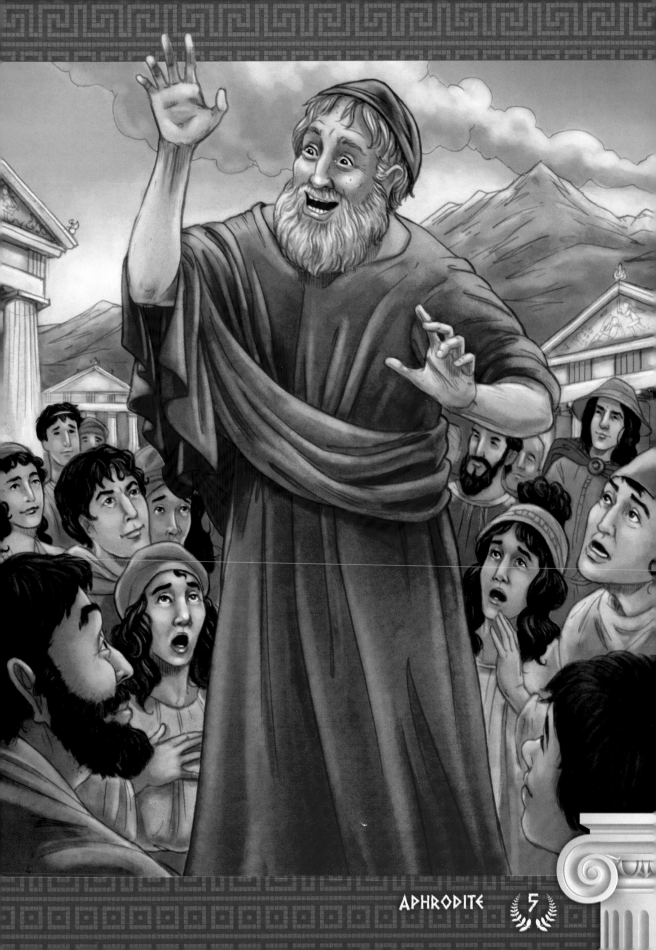

CHARACTERS AND PLACES

Mount Olympus
The mountaintop home of
the 12 Olympic gods

Aegean Sea

CRETE

ANCIENT GREECE

Cyprus
An Island in the Mediterranean and
the mythical home of Aphrodite.

Olympian Gods
Demeter, Hermes, Hephaestus,
Aphrodite, Ares, Hera, Zeus, Poseidon,
Athena, Apollo, Artemis, and Dionysus

Trojan War
War between the ancient
Greeks and Trojans

Adonis (uh-DOH-nis)
Handsome Greek youth killed by a boar;
loved by Aphrodite

Aphrodite (af-roh-DY-tee)
Goddess of love and beauty;
born of the sea foam; wife of
Hephaestus; mother of Eros

Ares (AIR-eez)
God of war; son of Zeus and Hera;
possible father of Eros

Atalanta (at-l-AN-tuh)
Greek heroine who fought with the
Argonauts; agreed to only marry the man
who could beat her in a footrace

Cronus (CROW-nus)
A Titan who ruled the world; married to
Rhea and their children became the first six
Olympic gods

Eros (AIR-ohs)
God of love; son of Aphrodite;
one of the original gods at the beginning
of creation

Gaea (JEE-uh)
Mother Earth and one of the first elements
born to Chaos; mother of the Titans,
Cyclopes, and Hecatoncheires

Helen (HEL-uhn)
Daughter of Zeus; her kidnapping by Paris
caused the Trojan War

Hephaestus (huh-FES-tuhs)
God of fire and metalwork; son of Zeus
and Hera; married to Aphrodite

Paris (PAR-is)
Trojan prince who caused the Trojan War
by kidnapping Helen

Pygmalion
(pig-MEY-lee-uhn)
Greek sculptor who fell in love
with his statue; Aphrodite
brought the statue to life

Uranus (YOO-ruh-nus)
The Sky and Heavens; born of Gaea along
with the mountains and seas; husband of
Gaea; father of the Titans, Cyclopes, and
Hecatoncheires

THE GODDESS OF LOVE AND BEAUTY

Aphrodite was the Greek goddess of love and beauty. She was also different from the other Olympic gods. Aphrodite alone had been born without a mother or father. The story of her birth was unique. It began at the beginning of time with the mighty Titans. The Titans were beautiful giants. They were the children of Gaea, or Mother Earth, and Uranus, the heavens and sky. The Titans represented the forces of nature.

Their father Uranus was ruler of the universe. He worried that his children would try to steal his power. He was right to worry. Uranus had confined some of his children in the underworld. This made Mother Earth upset. She tried to convince the Titans to rebel against Uranus. The only one brave enough to try was Cronus, the youngest of the Titans. Cronus received an unbreakable **sickle** from his mother to aid him in the battle. Cronus defeated Uranus with the blade and banished him from Earth. Uranus was injured during the fight. Cronus hurled the body parts he cut off Uranus over his shoulder. They scattered across the land and sea. Where the parts hit the sea, white foam formed. From the foam arose a beautiful **maiden**. This maiden was Aphrodite.

Aphrodite's name comes from the Greek word *aphros*, which means "foam".

APHRODITE

Zephyrus, the West Wind, greeted Aphrodite as dawn broke across the sky. Zephyrus gently blew Aphrodite toward the shore of the island of Cyprus. The Horae welcomed Aphrodite to the island. The Horae were three daughters of Zeus and represented the seasons and time. Everywhere Aphrodite stepped on the island, a flower bloomed. The Horae gave Aphrodite beautiful clothing and jewels. A wreath of roses was put on her flowing blonde hair. Aphrodite was placed into a golden chariot drawn by doves. She was then taken to meet the gods in their palace on Mount Olympus.

The Olympic gods were all amazed by Aphrodite's beauty. She was warmly welcomed to the palace in the clouds. Aphrodite was given a **throne** of gold. While Aphrodite was at the palace she began to perfect her skills as the goddess of love, beauty, and desire.

CYPRUS

Cyprus is the third largest island in the Mediterranean Sea. It is located off the southern coast of Turkey. Cyprus is known for its beautiful scenery. Mountains, lush fields, and beaches are just part of its appeal. In ancient times, Cyprus also had many raw minerals and produced excellent wines. Cyprus was thought to be the mythical home of Aphrodite.

Zeus, the king of the gods, soon worried that the other gods would fight over Aphrodite. Hera, Zeus's wife, knew the goddesses were jealous of Aphrodite's beauty. They agreed that something would have to be done about Aphrodite. The problem would soon be resolved.

Hephaestus was the lame and ugly god of fire. A lame person has difficulty walking because of an injury to the foot or leg. His body was not perfect like the other gods. Hephaestus had admired Aphrodite since the moment she arrived. But Hephaestus was sure he would never have a chance to win her favor. So he went about his business as **blacksmith** to the gods. But first he planned a little revenge for his mother, Hera. Hephaestus never forgot the cruel treatment he received from her at birth. He was lame because Hera had thrown him off Mount Olympus for being so ugly. Hephaestus created a beautiful throne to trick Hera. Hera could not resist the lovely gift. But as soon as she sat on it she was trapped. None of the other gods could figure out how to release her. They pleaded with Hephaestus to set Hera free, but he refused.

Then Dionysus, the god of wine, got Hephaestus drunk. This made Hephaestus finally agree to release Hera from the throne. Hephaestus drove a hard bargain though. He would only do so if Hera promised to give him Aphrodite as his wife. Hephaestus freed Hera and gained Aphrodite as his bride. Aphrodite was not happy.

There are many different symbols associated with Aphrodite, including the dove. The ancient city of Salamis in Cyprus marked its coins with this symbol.

Hephaestus wanted to make his wife happy. So he used all of his skills to create a magic girdle, or belt, for her. Aphrodite loved her gift, but it did not make her love her husband more. Instead, Aphrodite used her magic girdle to catch all sorts of men.

Aphrodite did not like the lame and ugly Hephaestus. She much preferred his more handsome brother Ares. Aphrodite and Ares began to meet in secret. They were sure they could keep Hephaestus in the dark about their affair. But Helios, the sun god, discovered their affair and told Hephaestus. Hephaestus was furious, so he created a magical net to trap the two gods. The net was made of fine links of **bronze** and was nearly invisible. Hephaestus cast his net over Aphrodite and Ares one night as they slept. Hephaestus then brought all the gods to judge the trapped pair. He hoped the embarrassment would cause Ares to end the affair. In the end, none of the gods could blame Ares. After all, who could resist Aphrodite's charm and beauty?

MAGIC GIRDLE

The girdle Hephaestus made for Aphrodite was made of the finest gold. Hephaestus also wove magic into the girdle's design. The girdle made all men fall hopelessly in love with its wearer. Combined with Aphrodite's beauty no one could resist its power.

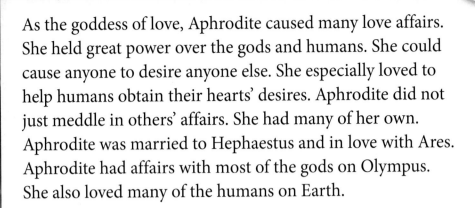

As the goddess of love, Aphrodite caused many love affairs. She held great power over the gods and humans. She could cause anyone to desire anyone else. She especially loved to help humans obtain their hearts' desires. Aphrodite did not just meddle in others' affairs. She had many of her own. Aphrodite was married to Hephaestus and in love with Ares. Aphrodite had affairs with most of the gods on Olympus. She also loved many of the humans on Earth.

These affairs produced many children. The most famous were her children with Ares. Together they had four children—three sons and a daughter. Phobos and Deimos were the gods of fear and terror. These twin sons were the constant companions of their father on the battlefields of war. Their daughter, the youthful goddess of harmony, was the exact opposite of her father. She was as lovely as her mother Aphrodite. The youngest child was Eros, the mischievous god of love.

PISCES CONSTELLATION

Pisces is a **constellation** in the northern sky. It is the twelfth sign of the zodiac. Ancient Greeks thought the stars in the constellation formed the shape of two fish. It was believed that the constellation represented Aphrodite and her son Eros. The two gods tried to flee from the monster Typhon. Typhon was the 100-headed son of Mother Earth. To escape, Aphrodite and Eros disguised themselves as fish. They tied their tails together so as not to get separated in the river. The Pisces constellation shows the two fish in the stars.

Aphrodite was a dazzling beauty. She was considered to be the perfect woman by ancient Greeks. She was often a bit conceited and used her beauty to catch men.

The Graces were Aphrodite's **attendants**. These three sister goddesses helped Aphrodite by giving beauty, charm, and goodness to young women. They also entertained the gods with their dancing. They spread joy wherever they went. The Erotes also accompanied Aphrodite. They were youthful winged gods of the various aspects of love. Himeros was the god of desire. Anteros was the god of love returned. Hymenaeus was the god of weddings.

Eros was Aphrodite's constant companion. Eros spent his time helping his mother interfere in the love affairs of gods and humans. His bow and arrows at the ready, Eros enjoyed shooting at the unsuspecting victims. His arrows could cause love, lack of interest, or even hatred. Aphrodite was often frustrated by the mischief Eros caused. Yet she asked for his help when interfering in others' love lives.

APHRODITE IN ART

One of the most famous paintings of Aphrodite is The Birth of Venus by Italian artist Sandro Botticelli. He was a famous artist from the fifteenth century AD. The painting shows a grown-up Venus standing in a seashell rising from the sea. Another example of Aphrodite in art is the ancient statue known as the Venus de Milo. Sculptor Alexandros of Antioch carved it around 150 BC. Aphrodite has been a popular subject for artists throughout the ages.

Aphrodite is credited with pairing some of the most famous lovers of all time. One story began with a contest. All of the gods and goddesses were invited to attend a wedding. Only Eris, the goddess of discord, was left out. Eris secretly went to the wedding to seek her revenge. While there, Eris threw her golden apple of discord into the crowd. Carved on the apple were the words, "For the Fairest." This caused a violent quarrel to break out between Hera, Athena (the goddess of war), and Aphrodite. Each claimed the apple and believed she was the fairest in the land. Zeus decided a judge was needed to settle the disagreement. Zeus chose Paris, the prince of Troy. But how was Paris to pick a winner?

The three goddesses set about trying to win Paris's favor. Hera promised Paris power. Athena promised the prince wisdom and victory in battle. But Aphrodite promised Paris the most beautiful woman in the world as his wife. It did not take Paris long to decide. He gave the golden apple to Aphrodite. Hera and Athena stormed off in anger. Aphrodite became Paris's friend and protector.

PYGMALION

Pygmalion was a sculptor in ancient Greece. He created a beautiful statue out of ivory. It was shaped like a woman. He named it Galatea. In prayer, Pygmalion asked the goddess Aphrodite for a wife as lovely as his statue. Aphrodite was delighted when she laid eyes on his lovely creation. Galatea looked just like Aphrodite! Aphrodite granted Pygmalion's wish and brought the statue to life. Galatea and Pygmalion fell in love instantly. They never forgot to thank Aphrodite for their good fortune.

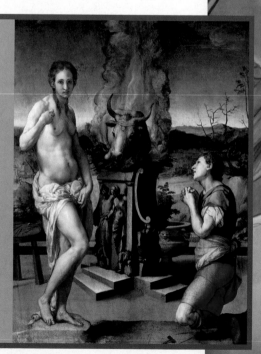

Aphrodite did not forget her promise to Paris. Helen was the stepdaughter of Tyndareus, the king of Sparta. She was the most beautiful woman in the world. There was just one problem with Aphrodite's plan. Helen was already married. Tyndareus had picked Menelaus as a husband for Helen. After Tyndareus's rule, Helen and Menelaus lived happily for many years as king and queen of Sparta. Then Aphrodite intervened.

Aphrodite convinced Eros to shoot Helen with one of his arrows of love. Eros's arrows worked their magic. Helen willingly left Sparta with Paris. Menelaus was furious. Leaders from all over Greece came together to form the greatest army of all time. It was the start of the Trojan War.

The gods had their hands full sorting out the mess Aphrodite had created. The war lasted ten long years. In the end, Paris was killed and Helen went back to live with Menelaus. Aphrodite helped Paris find love and beauty. He just did not get to enjoy it for very long.

ATALANTA

Atalanta was the swiftest maiden in the land. She would only marry the man who could beat her in a footrace. Hippomenes fell in love with Atalanta the first time he saw her run. He prayed to Aphrodite for help. Aphrodite appeared and gave Hippomenes three apples of pure gold. Hippomenes was to use them to distract Atalanta during their race. It worked perfectly. Atalanta stopped to pick up each apple that Hippomenes dropped. Hippomenes barely won the race but earned Atalanta as his bride.

Aphrodite was married to Hephaestus, but her one true love was his brother Ares. None of this stopped Aphrodite from noticing other men however. One unfortunate youth to catch her eye was Adonis. He was so beautiful as a baby that Aphrodite chose to protect him. She did not want the other goddesses to discover him, so she hid Adonis in a chest. Aphrodite then delivered him to Persephone, the queen of the underworld, to keep him safe. Persephone opened the chest and discovered the beautiful baby boy. When Aphrodite returned for Adonis, Persephone refused to give him up. Zeus was forced to resolve the problem. After hearing both sides Zeus declared that Adonis should spend half the year on Earth with Aphrodite. The other half would be spent in the underworld with Persephone. As the years passed, Adonis grew to be a very handsome man and Aphrodite fell in love with him.

Ares, the god of war, grew very jealous of Adonis. He decided to kill Adonis. Ares waited for a day when Adonis went out hunting alone. Ares then transformed himself into a giant boar and gored Adonis to death. Aphrodite mourned the loss of Adonis for a very long time.

WHY ROSES ARE RED

The red rose was a sacred flower to Aphrodite. When Adonis was killed she rushed to his side. In her hurry she cut her feet on the thorns of the roses nearby. As she knelt at Adonis's side, her blood dripped on the snow-white flowers. Ancient Greeks believed Aphrodite's blood created the red roses we have today.

Another human to surrender to Aphrodite's charms was Anchises, king of Dardania. Aphrodite did not start this affair with Anchises. Aphrodite was always interfering in the love lives of the other gods. She often teased them for falling under her love spells. Zeus decided to teach Aphrodite a lesson.

Zeus created a love spell for Aphrodite. So when Aphrodite spotted Anchises on Mount Ida, she fell madly in love with him. Aphrodite disguised herself as a human maiden and approached the king. Anchises soon gave in to Aphrodite's charms. Their affair produced a son named Aeneas. He was a great hero during the Trojan War. Aeneas was also the founder of Roman culture in Italy.

Aphrodite decided to reveal her true identity to Anchises. His reaction was not what Aphrodite expected. He was frightened. Anchises knew his relationship with Aphrodite would upset the other gods. Aphrodite told Anchises that this would not happen as long as he kept their affair a secret. But how could Anchises keep such wonderful news to himself? It did not take long for Anchises to brag about his affair with the goddess of love. As punishment, Zeus struck Anchises down with a thunderbolt.

In seventeenth century English, Aphrodite's name was pronounced to rhyme with the words *night* or *right*.

APHRODITE

Aphrodite was worshiped all over ancient Greece. She was especially popular in **Athens**, Corinth, and Cyprus. Worshipers came to her with their private prayers. They offered sacrifices of **incense**, flowers, and doves. Aphrodite could be generous in granting love to her followers. However, she was often cruel to those who neglected her worship.

Venus was the Roman goddess equal to Aphrodite. Romans believed Venus was the daughter of Jupiter, or Zeus. Cupid was her son. A great temple was built near the Colosseum and Roman Forum to honor Venus. Ancient Romans even named a planet after her. It seems fitting that the planet Venus is the brightest thing visible in the sky except the sun and the moon.

Ancient myths would have been dull without the added mischief of Aphrodite. Her beauty was legendary. And Aphrodite's interfering created some of the best love stories of all time. The goddess of love and beauty will continue to inspire love far into the future.

TEMPLE OF VENUS

The Temple of Venus was considered the largest temple in ancient Rome. The emperor and architect Hadrian commissioned it. The temple was dedicated to Venus in 135 AD. It was damaged by fire in 283 AD and again by earthquake in the ninth century AD. Today only a few columns remain. The remains can be viewed across from the Colosseum in Rome.

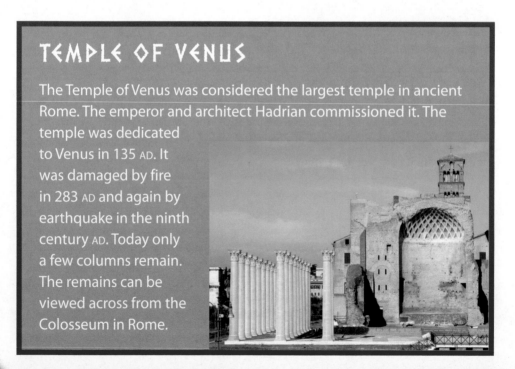

PRINCIPAL GODS OF GREEK MYTHOLOGY— A FAMILY TREE

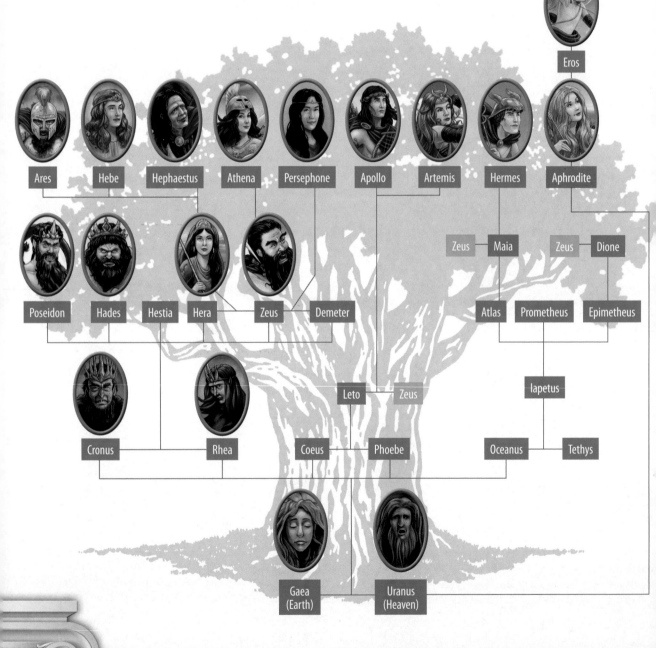

Eros

Ares | Hebe | Hephaestus | Athena | Persephone | Apollo | Artemis | Hermes | Aphrodite

Zeus — Maia | Zeus — Dione

Poseidon | Hades | Hestia | Hera — Zeus — Demeter | Atlas | Prometheus | Epimetheus

Iapetus

Cronus — Rhea | Leto — Zeus | Oceanus — Tethys

Coeus | Phoebe

Gaea (Earth) — Uranus (Heaven)

KEY WORDS

ancient Greece: historical period that lasted from about 800 to 323 BC, during which many advancements were made in politics, art, philosophy, and science

Athens: a busy and beautiful city in ancient Greece that is credited as the birthplace of democracy. Today, Athens is the largest city in Greece and is the country's capital

attendants: assistants or servants

blacksmith: someone who makes or repairs items made of iron

bronze: a yellowish-brown colored metal, made by combining tin and copper

constellation: a group of stars that creates a shape in the sky and has been given a name

incense: a substance that produces a strong, sweet smell when burned, often used in religious ceremonies

maiden: a girl or young woman who is not married

sickle: a tool with a short handle and a sharp, curved metal blade that is usually used for cutting grass or grains

throne: special chair for someone of power, such as a deity, king, or queen

worshiped: showed respect and honor, often through prayer or other religious acts

INDEX

Log on to www.av2books.com

AV² by Weigl brings you media enhanced books that support active learning. Go to www.av2books.com, and enter the special code found on page 2 of this book. You will gain access to enriched and enhanced content that supplements and complements this book. Content includes video, audio, weblinks, quizzes, a slide show, and activities.

AV² Online Navigation

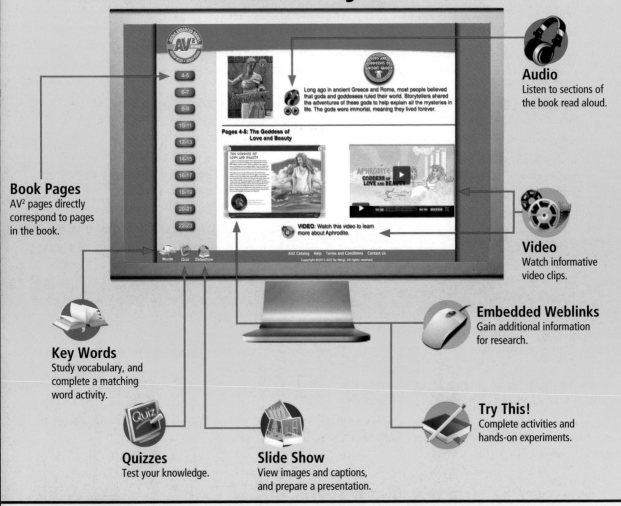

Audio
Listen to sections of the book read aloud.

Book Pages
AV² pages directly correspond to pages in the book.

Video
Watch informative video clips.

Embedded Weblinks
Gain additional information for research.

Key Words
Study vocabulary, and complete a matching word activity.

Try This!
Complete activities and hands-on experiments.

Quizzes
Test your knowledge.

Slide Show
View images and captions, and prepare a presentation.

AV² was built to bridge the gap between print and digital. We encourage you to tell us what you like and what you want to see in the future.

Sign up to be an AV² Ambassador at www.av2books.com/ambassador.